TRIBUTE NIGHT AT THE SOCIAL

*Dedicated to my wife
and our family and friends
with love*

TRIBUTE NIGHT AT THE SOCIAL

Peter Burgham

It's Open Mic Night !

Copyright © Peter Burgham 2020

The right of Peter Burgham to be identified as the author of this book has been asserted in accordance with the Copyright, Designs and Patents Act 1988.

First Printing: 2020

Reprint: 2023

ISBN 978-1-9163353-2-5   (paperback)

All rights reserved. No part of this publication may be reproduced, stored in a retrieval system, or transmitted, at any time or by any means (electronic, mechanical, photocopying, recording, or otherwise) without the prior written permission of the publisher.

Published by: Peter Burgham
                York, England

A CIP catalogue record for this book is available from the British Library.

Website: www.burg34.com

TRIBUTE NIGHT AT THE SOCIAL

All-Star Cast List

Poem: *Performer:*

In The Bar Afterwards   **Roger McGough**
Somewhere Between an Orange
and Tesco's   **Brian Patten**
A Useless Tale   **Ian McMillan**
Owd Wenches   **Liz Berry**
Voices   **Hugo Williams**
Circle of Life   **Mona Arshi**
The Crown   **Rudyard Kipling**
Community   **George The Poet**
Delphinium   **Ted Kooser**
Breakout   **TS Eliot**
Sad Shires   **Wilfred Owen**
Armpit Lane   **Helen Mort**
Dem Pomes   **John Bishop**
I Imagine You Sometimes   **Mersey Poets**

(Host/Comedian)   **Billy Connolly**

Bannockpace is my fictional Scottish town.

Each poem is a homage to the celebrity, in the manner of a TV impressionist or musical tribute act. And as with those acts, some tributes may work better than others, and any resemblance may be purely coincidental!

It's Tribute Night
here at

**Bannockpace
Sports & Social Club**

so listen up people !

We've got something a wee bit different for yer tonight.

Poetry - it's the new Rock 'n' Roll.

So give it up fer these lads and lassies.

*First up is national treasure, **Roger McGough**.*
He hasn't been knighted yet, as far as I know, but surely only a matter of time...

In The Bar Afterwards

I want to shake the hand
of the man who shook the hand of

Gandhi	(GK)
Kennedy	(RB)
Gorbachev	(LB)
Mandela	(RH)
Einstein	(CH)
Bradman	(LH)
Shakespeare	(OR)
Presley	(IR)
Churchill	(CF)
Picasso	(IL)
do Nascimento	(OL)

and any of the other lads who played for
Gianthammer United, 1963-78.

Good mates. Good times.

Buffet's open folks. Help yourself to the cheese straws, pal.

Next up, a double act:
*"A cocktail of **Patten** and **McGough**, a Mersey Martini."*
Down in one then lads...

Somewhere Between an Orange and Tesco's

I borrowed an orange without asking
and kept it in my pocket
and everywhere I went
I offered it to passers-by.

But no-one would take my orange
they said it wasn't quite good enough
they needed something easier
like fate or grass or life.

They said why couldn't I offer cherry or pear
but all I had was orange.
Why should it be so hard to offer
an orange ?

How is it as you grow older
it becomes more and more difficult to accept
that orange will not do, that there is
no rhyme for orange ?

Vodka anyone ?
Anyone ... these fellers need a rhyme for vodka.

Ah here's Barnsley's favourite bard, **Ian McMillan**, who's dropped by to give us some Yorkshire words of wisdom.

A Useless Tale

Don't use a thimble to drink up your ale,
Don't use a gloved hand to read words in braille,
Don't use a chipmunk to make a Chippendale,
Don't use an ice cube to carve out a dale,
Don't use an e-stamp to send an e-mail,
Don't use any excuse to constantly fail,
Don't use a straw house to weather the gale,
Don't use a paper hat to fend off the hail,
Don't use a hairpin as a means to impale,
Don't use a real card to get out of jail,
Don't use a kake to mix with your kale,
Don't use a penknife to harvest your lale,
Don't use female logic to understand the male,
Don't use a pencil to hammer in your nail,
Don't use a hot bath to boil your oxtail,
Don't use a plaster to fix holes in your pail,
Don't use a pit lamp to dazzle a quail,
Don't use a toothbrush to paint up your rail,
Don't use a Ferrari to overtake a snail,
Don't use an arrow to pin the donkey's tail,
Don't use an ode to an un-nightingale,
Don't use a cloud to float over your vale,
Don't use a fishhook to capture a whale,
Don't use an ex-glass to drink your ex-ale,
Don't use a hatchet to unpick your Yale,
Don't use a chainsaw to prune your azal-ea,
Except to get in the Guinness Book of Records.

I'm sure some of them words are just made-up.

Here's someone else wi' a local voice and a special style, **Liz Berry**. *Hope we can understand that accent, duck.*

Owd Wenches

Come wenches from Tipton along the cut
past the bone orchard at Frosty Hill,
haunted by mardy owd girls
lowping like foxes in the woods,
come swiftly past the locks at Dudley,
come looking fer the west wind, come
feathered me ducks and roll amongst the ferns
and sweet petunias, come darkly down the road
collied by sleet and shining like coal.

There's bostin fittle at this party, faggits
and pays and jugs of amber nectar,
wenches and lads kaylighed and canting
like binlids in an alley gust.
Come starry nightowls, come hither
and chap the moon.

Hmmm... my Sat Nav disnae mention any bone orchard.

Next guy's the only one in here who's had a car named after him. Gi'it some laldy, **Yugo** *...*

Voices

I rang your phone several times
today. Your automated message
trailed off into the distance
like a stick thrown for a dog.

Later when you answered
I heard background noise
like those old party lines,
laughter and music,

...business meeting... late...
bad line... miss you...
ciao, amore......

fading in and out,
losing the connection.

Now then girls, is that a custard tart or a meringue ?

Adding her own distinctive voice to proceedings, here's
Mona Arshi.

Circle of Life

Catch the beauty of a hummingbird,
let it slip beneath your surface,
cast away the mantle of your sorrow.

Let the feathered iridescence
of amethyst, ruby and emerald illuminate
your grey skies like a jewelled rainbow.

Let the small coin
perched on your outstretched palm
be the weight of your world.

Small coin? Aye, d'ye remember them...the heated pennies ?

*And now, well, we have a real legend, **Rudyard Kipling**. You've got one minute, son.*

The Crown

I once found a crown half-hidden in the sand
A jewel amongst bare stones
Shielded from the ebb of the pounding sea
Sunken treasure sun-kissed on the periphery
    Of a raking eye.

A fresh breeze whipping up the guardian shore
Laid bare the precious metal
Curiosity tempting this boy who would be king,
Brave steps to the verge of that silvery something
    Imagination wild and free.

A bold lunge forward, Excalibur grasped,
Sand-grit fingers scraping at the rim.
Grain by grain revealing its tint,
Then held up high to the sun, a magical glint
    Foretelling of a princely sum.

Back home, the treasure was safely stowed,
From time to time unwrapped
To stand and gaze in awe at its imperial rule,
Until one dark evening after proud display at school,
    Coming home, it slipped away unseen.

Sorry tae interrupt there big man - burgers are up. Special tonight - 2 fer the price of 1, but dinnae all rush, keep yer heid on. Right, carry on, pal...

The Crown, cont'd...

> A lost kingdom, an irreplaceable token,
> It was the silver-gilt symbol of my realm,
> Worth more than anyone could ever earn,
> I'd have paid a king's ransom for its return,
>   This was the End of Empire.
>
> And the moral of this simple tale:
> Life can revolve on a coin that's tossed,
> But if in time you can treat your fate
> With equal weight as Kipling meant,
> The treasure stored, the treasure spent,
>   You'll be the King of the Castle, my Son.

You should try the cakes too, Mr K.

*Next, speaking up for the community, it's **George the Poet**.*

Community

My city is amazing
a jangle of people wherever you're gazing
a jungle a zoo or whatever angle you're raising,
kids on the street bright-eyed, stargazing
parents with pride, coping and praising.

But some not so star-blessed
kids on the street blank-eyed and lazing
kids in the dock blazing, hell-raising, half-crazing,
landlords and bosses hell-bent, half-assed and hazing.

But look deeper - young helping old, old helping young
black and white breaking down barriers and liaising,
and one day the rich no longer stealing from the poor,
the money no longer buried deep offshore, one day
one day - we call this faith, we call it trail-blazing.

The news is all around you
not just on TV
not just in soundbites fed to the community
by executives with immunity
from images of reality
where truth becomes a rarity.
At the end of the day
the news is you and you and you and me.

It's time for re-appraising.
My city is amazing.

Respect, Mr the P.

And a special guest from America, **Ted Kooser**.

Delphinium

The flowers have withered in this cemetery
in Red Barn Creek where once they framed
the path with hummingbirds hovering
like a line of rifles forming a guard of honor
for the mourners and the passing coffin.

In the distance a train whistle repeats,
sending its condolence on the wings of larks
across the bowing wheatfields of Nebraska,
beyond the faded orange and purple delphi
to the steps of the church.

Hailstones descend on the flowers
strewn like weary old soldiers
awaiting their turn to shake
the dead hand of the frost.

Thanks for that Ted. You can get back tae yer lectures now...

This feller's name can form 112 words in Scrabble...
Gaun yersen, **L.I. Totes** *...*

Breakout

time inside	is	like a solitary drip falling unending to a concrete end
the end	is freedom freedom is	the end of time
freedom then	is	outside time another dimension
time	with	the floodgates opened unstoppable but stopping freely
time	to	look inside
time	to	look outside
time	to	look beyond
fly	said	the jailbird
fly	to	the ocean's edge where time flattens time time stops but never ends

---

Time fer a drink, pal.

Breakout, cont'd...

time past	is	infinite paradigms of how it was and how it might have been
time future	is	infinite unknown but known and tolls the same for you and me
time now	is	on the edge of infinity ticking louder and louder in an endless chain of silence
time	will	end
freedom	will	end
the chain	will	be broken

Is that the last bell?

*Next up, **Wilfred Owen**. He's got a wee poem about smoking or some such thing. There was a lot of smoke in his day.*

Sad Shires

In a year when sinister smoke filled the sky,
When, despite what you saw, did you understand why ?
As you charged through the valleys of death in the shires,
With pointing of fingers and screeching of tyres,
At the dawning of the two-car Age,
Into the new Millennium with the same old Rage,
In the midst of the phoney fast-lane battle,
What passing horns were sounded for those dying cattle ?
What lights for the burning fields and the rotting piles ?
What thoughts beyond the guy in front and the business
                                                        miles ?

In a year when sinister smoke filled the sky,
When the new world shook, when we saw so many die,
As the agents of death charged through skyscraper valleys,
When fingers were pointed at the wailing disease,
At the dawning of the new crusade,
Into the new Apocalypse rattling the same old blade,
In the midst of the cries of infidel and vengeance,
What bells were tolled for the passing of innocence ?
Did you spare a thought for the world today,
As you cursed the people who got in your way ?

A friend of mine barged through the traffic the other day...
I didn't even know he had a boat...

Now here's a lassie who kens her way roond a word factory,
Helen Mort.

Armpit Lane

The wardens lock up the pawn shop,
head for home past the cathedral's
blue cantilever stand. Birds line the roof,
chanting vespers. Darkness falls.
The black grille awaits the onslaught,
tense as Sheffield steel. Outside
on the street the inmates gather,
scanning the gutters for silver,
the end of the lane for copper.
A brick is thrown in hope,
rebounds as a laugh.
Magpies. Jewels. Sirens.
Black-and-white case.

Ye'd huv tae rename that as 'Oxter Lane' in Scotland.
One for the road, hen?

*It wouldnae be a party wi'oot a wee gatecrasher. Here's Scouse comedian **John Bishop**, getting into the spirit.*

Dem Pomes

Dem pomes dem pomes is in me 'ead
And softly through my dreams de tread

De ravel out dem mental knots
Give t's the cross and i's the dots

And like dem sparklers de crackle in me mind
Pyrotechnux of the cerebral kind

De take me to a magic place
Take inner fears to outer space

And like da stars yer carn explain
Nor wrap dem up in cellophane

I know yer think dat rhymes are sad
And youse may say 'been on da waccy lad?'

But let me tell yer this my friend
Da first sign of madness is when dem pomes end.

It's the way yer tell 'em, pal. Lang may yer lum reek, JB.

*So now we come to our last act. It's the **Mersey Poets** again. They get everywhere...*

> ### I Imagine You Sometimes
>
> I imagine you sometimes
> in the lead crystal of my glass
> still looking good
> I see you kissing
> a man a magnumofchampagne
> rollerattheraces man
> and holding hands
> you walk towards the bedroom
> but when the lights go out
> I can't see you
> any more
> so I refill with whisky
> and try to get to the bottom of things.

Well it's been an absolutely er ... different ... evening.

Talking of different, next week we've got a pie-eating contortionist act from Romania. Tickets still available.

Bar shuts tonight in twenty minutes, form a queue behind them poets.

And I'll leave yer with this thought:

How is it that the triangular sandwiches always taste better than the square ones ?

It's not what's in your loaf, folks, it's how you cut it.

ACKNOWLEDGEMENTS

Tribute Night at the Social originally achieved recognition in the Yeovil 'Writing Without Restrictions' competition, where it was awarded 3rd prize in 2017.

The version here has some minor improvements, plus some new material.

Judge Kiran Millwood Hargrave commented:

"A sure-footed and witty take-off of a poet's rite of passage: the open mic. The writer wonderfully ventriloquises poets from McGough to TS Eliot..."

Note:
Bannockpace Sports & Social Club is my fictional venue. Any similarity to any real location would be coincidental.

Also by the same author:

BIRD'S EYE VIEW

PAUSE AND REWIND (series)

CONNECTIONS : Railway Verses

More poetry and verse and links to other creative arts can be found on:

www.burg34.com

www.ingramcontent.com/pod-product-compliance
Lightning Source LLC
Chambersburg PA
CBHW071759080526
44588CB00013B/2307